LIKE ME

28 DAYS TO CONFIDENCE, CLARITY, AND SELF-LOVE

INGRID JAMES

INGRID JAMES

LIKE ME

28 DAYS

TO CONFIDENCE, CLARITY, AND SELF-LOVE

Blalton
PUBLISHERS LLC

Like Me
28 Days to Confidence, Clarity, and Self-Love

Copyright © 2025 by Ingrid James

All rights reserved.

Printed in the United States of America

Print ISBN: 978-1-940698-37-3

Published by Biblion Publishing
Suwanee, GA

Unless otherwise indicated, scripture quotations are taken from the
Holy Bible, especially, the English Standard Version (ESV), and the
New International Version (NIV).

CONTENTS

HOW TO GET THE MAXIMUM BENEFITS FROM THIS BOOK

To set the stage, read the first six sections.

- Read the day pages in order, along with the following:
  - Reflection Exercise
  - Inspirational Quote
  - And the Mental and Physical Activity that correlates with each day.

PURPOSE

This book is designed to give you 28 days of mental exercises to help you release negative thinking that can obstruct your positive progress as you navigate the ups and downs of your life's journey. Throughout the book, I provide visual adaptations that allow you to view the world and your experiences with an optimistic lens, keep situations in the proper perspective, and promote a newfound way to experience self-love.

I hope this book will transform lives, develop character, and reshape the landscape of an entire generation that currently defines self-esteem through social media.

When life's environment has you in a place where you are motivated by fear, you develop thoughts and habits that can lead to unhealthy character traits that you must now undo. To change one's life course, you must first address the root cause of those deeply embedded fears.

There are choices in life… Give up, give in, or give it all you've got! So, if you have thought about the first two but want the last one. Take this simple step and dedicate the next 28 days to Romans 12:2.

> *Do not conform to the pattern of this world but be transformed by the renewing of your mind.* - Romans 12:2

DEDICATION

I dedicate this book to my son Joshua and my family in remembrance of the Poem "If" by Rudyard Kipling; that my mom recited to us, on her deathbed.

"IF"
By Rudyard Kipling

If you can keep your head when all about you
Are losing theirs and blaming it on you,
If you can trust yourself when all men doubt you,
But make allowance for their doubting too;
If you can wait and not be tired by waiting,
Or being lied about, don't deal in lies,
Or being hated, don't give way to hating,
And yet don't look too good, nor talk too wise:

If you can dream—and not make dreams your master;

If you can think—and not make thoughts your aim;
If you can meet with Triumph and Disaster
And treat those two impostors just the same;
If you can bear to hear the truth you've spoken
Twisted by knaves to make a trap for fools,
Or watch the things you gave your life to, broken,
And stoop and build 'em up with worn-out tools:

If you can make one heap of all your winnings
And risk it on one turn of pitch-and-toss,
And lose, and start again at your beginnings
And never breathe a word about your loss;
If you can force your heart and nerve and sinew
To serve your turn long after they are gone,
And so hold on when there is nothing in you
Except the Will which says to them: 'Hold on!'

If you can talk with crowds and keep your virtue,
Or walk with Kings—nor lose the common touch,
If neither foes nor loving friends can hurt you,
If all men count with you, but none too much;
If you can fill the unforgiving minute
With sixty seconds' worth of distance run,
Yours is the Earth and everything that's in it,
And—which is more—you'll be a Man, my son!

INTRODUCTION

Take a chance on yourself, because you are worth it!

Heavenly Father,

The desired intent of writing this book is to create a useful tool for building up your kingdom. I want to help others understand how to strengthen their self-love and self-esteem without the need for external "likes", attention, and the approval of others. Furthermore, I wish to equip people with how to maintain a positive state of mind despite facing seeming troubles. May the reader find the structure and discipline of using this 28-day journey impactful and it becomes a catalyst that ignites a deeper sense of self-love.

THE PIT: EXPECT TO GROW EVEN IN DARKNESS

Sometimes, life places you in a cold, dark, and isolating space. It may feel unfair, overwhelming, or even unbearable. But know this—when God is ready to birth something new in your life, He often plants you in a pit. The depth of your pit isn't a punishment; it's preparation. The weaker your mind, faith, or strength at that moment, the deeper your pit may seem. Strong seeds require only shallow pits. Delicate seeds need deeper ones to be properly fortified.

We all experience seasons of both strength and weakness. Sometimes, God's timing aligns with our weakest moments, placing us in a deeper pit for a reason. And as counterintuitive as it may sound, that deep pit is exactly where you want to be.

A deep pit shields your opportunity seed from external threats. A faint wind won't blow it away. Heavy rain won't wash it away. Predators won't carry it off. What looks like struggle is actually protection. God surrounds your seed with dirt, sometimes in the form of difficult people, misjudgments, closed doors, or painful setbacks. But that dirt isn't there to bury you; it's there to fortify your growth.

How people treat you is a reflection of them: how you choose to respond is a reflection of you. You must develop resilience and an immunity to the negativity and opinions of others. You may not be able to control external circumstances, but you *can* control what happens within you. And when the time is right, the very dirt that once covered you will become the soil that nourishes your growth.

THE STRESS TEST

Think about this: Stress cannot be seen or placed in a box. It is only our views of what is happening that create stressful thinking.

In life, God will give you Seeds in the form of a purpose, a destiny, a plan, a desire, or a calling. God will allow water to come; it may feel like it's drowning your seed. It may come down so forcefully that it pushes even more dirt on top of you and your seed. You are so deep in the pit now you cannot see any light. No way out. No light at the end of your path. This then, is the time God needs you to stay still and increase your true faith, to hold on to God's word, even when you cannot see your own way out. Stay steadfast in prayer and the reading of His word.

When the outer shell of your seed breaks open and peels off, you may feel even more vulnerable and exposed.

The thin outer layer, the coating that fell off, is the old you; it is your old way of thinking, approaching things, doing things. So, it had to come off. Because the NEW you has gotten bigger and stronger inside, that old you must change. As soon as you try to move, God will begin to tie you down and anchor you in the soil with sprouted roots. These openings in your seed will also allow nutrients from the soil to enter you and the seed. Know He is feeding and strengthening you. Remember the roots have now tied you down and anchored you, so BE Still. This is so you cannot escape or run away from your destiny, your calling.

It's no doubt hard to be still and wait in the dark, buried in a pit. Knowing you have a gift. Know that you are brilliant, know that you deserve better, and know that you have the seed of opportunity. Not seeing the how, the when, or the where. Wet, tired, and anchored to the soil. I call it your Job season.

This is where your faith is tested and increased.

This is where your heart is tested and increased.

This is when your mind is tested and increased.

This is when your actions are tested.

Understand this season must come; God needs you to be strong enough to hold onto and keep your purpose once it manifests in your life. This season defines and builds your true character.

Your Courage,

Your Resilience,

Your Will,

This season is designed to strengthen your mental muscle, so learn, store up knowledge, remember wisdom, and be able to access it again and again when needed. This wisdom, when applied, will help you navigate through future situations and circumstances. So, remember the test season and the endurance you acquired while you were going through your Job season.

Once you pass this test, your root system is established, and your foundation is forming, which will give you the strength to grow in your purpose.

EMERGING

When you first break through the soil in your purpose, you look up and see the sun. Then you look down and see the pit and the soil you've been in, and you establish a new and deeper understanding, purpose, and respect for this initial growth stage. As you grow up and outward, you look different because you have transformed. Start making steps toward the direction of your destiny/ purpose. Mini accomplishments over time.

To train your brain, you must press/work past perceived obstacles and negative thoughts by reevaluating how you view the perceived negativity and changing your perspective to purposeful positive thoughts of growth. Relinquishing *the how* you get to the end result.

Grapes must be CRUSHED to make wine.
Diamonds form under the PRESSURE of the dirt.
Olives are PRESSED to release olive oil.
Seeds grow in DARKNESS.
Whenever you feel crushed, under pressure, pressed, or in darkness,
Know that you are in a ***powerful place,*** where God can transform you!
Trust the process! Trust God!

What defines you? Your character, your self-esteem, your self-love, your confidence.

If you let "likes" on social media dictate what you do and don't do, what you say and don't say, or what you wear and don't wear, you will never truly know who *you* are. Allowing social media to shape your identity means surrendering your uniqueness to strangers, people who have never met you, who don't truly know you, and who certainly don't know the purpose, destiny, or desires God has placed in your heart. Your destiny is *yours*, not theirs. Your dreams, your goals, your purpose, they belong to *you*.

Social media should never define you. Neither should Xbox, PlayStation, video games, or even the opinions of friends. And while your parents may help guide you, even they cannot define who you are meant to become.

God will shape you, but *you* define you. It's called *self*-esteem for a reason, it is the esteem of *oneself.* Love who you are. Love your style, your smile, your hobbies, and the unique way you see the world. Embrace the things that make you, *you.*

THE MIRROR CHALLENGE

Take a moment. Find a mirror. Look at yourself for three minutes—completely uninterrupted. No phone. No internet. No distractions. Just *you*.

Look deeper. What do you see? *Who* do you see? Do you like what you see?

Look beyond the surface. See your character. See your heart. Examine your actions, your words, and the way you treat others. Now ask yourself, do you like what you see?

You *should* like what you see, flaws, mistakes, and all. Because *you* are a work in progress, and you always have the power to grow and evolve. You can upgrade yourself, refine yourself, and improve yourself, but through it all, you must continue to love the foundation of who you are.

What you post, share, and do should be because *you* love it, not because you're chasing approval. Usually people only post the good things, the best version of themselves, not showing the struggles you went through to get where you are. Sometimes it is a façade. If no one taps the like button, would you still post it? Would you still share it? Would you still pursue it? If the answer is yes, then you are living authentically.

But remember, not everything needs to be shared, especially when it's still in a fragile state. Some aspects of your life are meant to be nurtured privately before being displayed publicly.

Your value is not tied to a like; it is tied to your character.

Your value is not tied to the like; it is tied to your character.

I want you to gaze at yourself for 2-3 minutes each day. Just stop and stare at you. You should begin to see things about you that you didn't even know. Say hello and good morning to yourself. Say something caring to yourself each morning. Speak a word of encouragement to yourself while looking in the mirror.

BABY ROOTS

Your roots are still young and small, and at times, they may be exposed. You might find yourself quick to anger, speaking with sharp words before thinking. But when someone comes along and highlights a weakness, resist the urge to retaliate. Instead, train your mind to recognize: *Aah, that's a weakness I now see one I can overcome.*

Pause and ask yourself: *Why did that upset me? Was it true? Is it tied to something in my past that I've been working to leave behind?* This is a moment for honesty. Reflection will give you the ability to grow.

Put it into perspective: *Is it still true today? Or have I matured beyond it? Is it something I still need to work on? Or is it merely a perception?*

Growth begins when you stop reacting and start reflecting.

HOW YOU SEE IT, WHERE TRUE BEAUTY LIES

Where is beauty first noticed? On the outside. But where does beauty last? On the inside.

Your outer self attracts, but your inner self keeps. Makeup, muscles, and stylish clothes may catch someone's eye, but your attitude, drive, and ethics determine whether they stay. What you *say* might attract, but what you *do* keeps. Showing up might create an opportunity, but putting in the work sustains it. And by now, you should realize I'm not just talking about relationships.

What dictates your choices? Who dictates them?

Some of us need to cut the puppet strings in our lives. You are *not* a puppet on a string, controlled by social media, peer pressure, or the expectations of others. Your life is yours to define. And when you cut the strings, don't throw away the wood; it's shaped like a cross. Lean on it. Lean on God. He will help you stand tall, strong, and unwavering in your purpose.

DAY 1

CLAIMING YOUR DESIRES

MORNING CHARGE:

Grind.

Some things come easily. Some things are hard. And some things take practice.

There is more than one way to achieve your goals. If the first path doesn't work, look beyond the obvious. There is always another way. Don't let obstacles stop you, frustrate you, or block your success and happiness. Instead, view them as detours guiding you to a better route. The universe may be offering a path you hadn't considered, one that is more aligned with your purpose.

Negative Disease #1: DISTRACTION

Dis-traction is anything designed to stop your flow, hinder your forward progress, and break your traction.

When you are distracted, you lose momentum. Your energy becomes scattered, and your focus shifts away from what truly matters.

Sometimes, distractions appear as obstacles, but in reality, they are redirections. God's plan may not always align with your own, but that doesn't mean it's not the best route. Let go of the need to control *how* you get there, as long as you get there. When you release attachment to *your* way, you align with divine flow, allowing things to unfold with effortless ease.

Remember: "For my thoughts are not your thoughts, neither are your ways my ways, declares the Lord." (Isaiah 55:8)

Trust that the journey is unfolding as it should. Stay committed, stay focused, and keep moving forward.

Reflection Exercise:

- Identify one area where you feel stuck. Is there another approach you haven't considered?

- What distractions have been pulling you away from your goals? How can you refocus?

AFFIRMATION:

I release the need to control how my success unfolds. I trust that everything is working in my favor. I stay focused, undeterred, and aligned with my divine purpose.

I am open to the new and changing. Every moment presents a great opportunity to become more of who I am. I am in flow with life, I am flexible, and therefore I can handle life changes effortlessly.

PHYSICAL ACTIVITY (GRATITUDE & SELF-LOVE):

Mirror, Mirror, on the wall, it's day 1 = here's looking at you! Look and have a caring conversation with yourself for 3 minutes. Remember to look deeply, not just at the surface of what you see.

Stand in front of a mirror and say out loud one thing you desire in your life. Speak it with confidence and visualize yourself achieving it.

MINDFUL EXERCISE:

Take 5 minutes to meditate on your goals and desires. Visualize them coming to life. As you focus, ask God to guide you in achieving them and believing it is possible.

BIBLICAL PASSAGE:

> *"Ask and it will be given to you; seek and you*
> *will find; knock and the door will be opened*
> *to you."* — Matthew 7:7

God is ready to fulfill your desires, but you must ask, believe, and trust in His timing. Note: The desires you seek, must align with God's good and perfect will.

DAY 2
EMBRACE THE VICISSITUDES OF LIFE

MORNING CHARGE:

All things work together for your greatness.

The growth and evolution of the mind are essential. Universal evolution is required for survival.

As you grow, you must evolve, change, adapt, let go of certain things, embrace new ones, shift your vantage point, and adjust your perspective. Where there is stagnation, there is no growth—only decline.

Nature provides countless examples: plants and animals adapt to survive, and humans, too, must recognize and embrace change at every stage of life. Sometimes, this means doing more or less of something to achieve the results you seek. Perhaps it's time to go deeper in your prayer life. Perhaps it's time to let go and prune away what no longer serves you. Be keenly aware: everything is subject to change.

Things that have run their course will come to an end. Celebrate that and let them go.

When you resist the natural changes that God is guiding you through, you are resisting the flow of the universe itself. And that, my friend, is an exhausting battle. Instead, embrace change, even when you don't fully understand it, because almost always, on the other side of transformation, is a new and improved version of YOU. So, take courage and move forward. Get there, get there, get there.

Hint: Don't dwell on your past. Don't beat yourself up over what you used to do. Maybe it wasn't ideal at the time, but it may have been a necessary experience to prepare you for what's next, equipping you for your journey.

Take your time. Sometimes, after being down for so long, you don't even realize that God has already begun lifting you. Your circumstances have shifted, and change is unfolding around you. Be patient. Trust the process. Even when you don't see progress or question why things are happening the way they are, know this:

In time, you will understand why these changes were necessary for your growth, your purpose, and your evolution.

Mental Activity:

Review what you are doing now. Journal it. Then review the list and do the following:

1. Delegate something off your list
2. Remove something from the list
3. Keep something on the list
4. Change how you deal with something on that list.
5. Revisit a challenge that is occurring
6. I am in flow with. . .

Remember, evolution is necessary for survival. Peaks and valleys exist in our lives for a purpose. There is wisdom to gain from your peaks and your valleys. Don't try to sidestep them, avoid them, or go around them, because you might miss the important tool God is trying to equip you with that will be key to your destiny.

Your destiny is too important to give up for anything or anyone. In fact, you owe it to the world to live up to what God called you to do! The world needs your gift.

AFFIRMATION:

"I accept that growth comes through change. I evolve, adapt, and welcome new experiences as part of my journey."

PHYSICAL ACTIVITY (GRATITUDE & SELF-LOVE):

Stretch for five minutes, thanking your body for its ability to carry you through your daily tasks. Feel the strength and flexibility you possess.

MINDFUL EXERCISE:

Write down a challenge you are currently facing. Now, list at least one lesson or positive takeaway you can gain from it. This shift in perspective is key to embracing life's changes.

BIBLICAL PASSAGE:

> *"For I know the plans I have for you, declares the Lord, plans to prosper you and not to harm you, plans to give you hope and a future."* — Jeremiah 29:11

Remember, God's plans for you are always for your good, even when it feels like life is uncertain.

DAY 3
MIND SELF-TALK

⸺◦◦❦◦◦⸺

MORNING CHARGE:

You have what it takes on the inside of you, so show me with your outward actions.

Your brain is always monitoring and spying on your thoughts. Guard them because your brain is always eavesdropping.

Diseases of the brain are:

Dis-traction – when you allow things to take you off track of your goals and objectives, talk you out of doing what God called you to do.

Neglect – brought on by years of wrong thought patterns taught, experienced, or the lack of experience. And past pain.

Indecisive – in different, don't care, numb to real feelings, bottled up feelings, fear so you don't act. Mentally lazy, hiding your head in the sand.

Doubt/ worry / Fear – lack faith and knowing who you belong to, spiritually weak; fear-based is object referral where you need someone or something to validate who you are.

Overcautious – think too much, overthinking, need all the facts and blessing of others before you act or do, adverse to all risk, asking others for confirmation.

Pessimistic - looking at things from the negative side; finds fault, why things won't work, feeds on negative situations and seems to enjoy negative things, reads negative news first.

Procrastination – no action, delaying action, putting off acting.

Do you find your thoughts fall into one of these categories? If you answered yes, you are not alone. This is a constant battle for many. You must quiet your inner turbulence.

Poor thinking makes you poor, it's not your work habits.

Every day, you must stand guard at the door of your mind.

Have you ever said, I am just having a bad day?

Truth is, did you really have a bad day, or did you have a bad 10-minute situation? The 10 to 20 minutes dragged on because you called your friend and shared what happened. In that moment you relived it and probably got upset all over again.

The truth is, YOU let your thoughts and the actions of others run undisciplined in your mind. Which led you to think you were having a bad day. It may have been a bad vibe, a bad interaction, a bad 10-minute situation, negative words spoken to you or about you, or a bad moment that YOU allowed to dwell with you throughout the whole day.

Come on... You run, you. It's called self-control and self-esteem for a reason. You let it in and allowed it to fester in your mind, body, and day. So, pay attention to how you let outside things influence and dictate what is happening on the inside of you. ***Don't give it real estate in your mind.*** Negativity likes to dump itself on others. Don't be a dumping ground for other people's negativity.

I will repeat it again: guard your mind!

Every time you hear negative self-talk talking (give it a name) and say _____ stop, stop right there. You are wrong, and I am not allowing you to talk to me today. That is wrong, NO.

AFFIRMATION:

"My thoughts shape my reality. Today, I chose to speak kindness and encouragement to myself."

PHYSICAL ACTIVITY (GRATITUDE):

Meditate for 10 minutes before bed and just after any **perceived** stressful *event*.

Take in 3 deep breaths, hold for a moment, and breathe out slowly.

Focus on **1** positive thought and 1 positive place you've **been**.

Monitor digital distractions. Set time limits on them. For 30 minutes, I will scroll through TikTok or Snap, set your phone alarm for 30 minutes, and when the alarm goes off - STOP.

MINDFUL EXERCISE:

Before going to bed, meditate for 10 minutes. Take deep breaths, hold for a moment, and release slowly. Focus on a positive memory or moment that brings you joy.

BIBLICAL PASSAGE:

"Finally, brothers and sisters, whatever is true,

whatever is noble, whatever is right,
whatever is pure, whatever is lovely,
whatever is admirable—if anything is
excellent or praiseworthy—think about such
things." — Philippians 4:8

Fill your mind with positive, uplifting thoughts, as they are the seeds of your actions.

DAY 4
METANOIA AWAKENING

―❦―

MORNING CHARGE:

Do you believe in you, because I do!

Cement Boots. Do you feel stuck and cannot get out from under? Does it feel like you are wearing cement boots? How do you get out from under, how do you gain the courage to get out of bed, move on, and simply get a good night's rest? How do you find time for you? How do you get your Diva / Swagger back?

Have you said I just don't know what to do? Three steps forward, two steps back. . .

I am here to tell you that yes, you do. Force yourself to come up with something. Write it down. Then, set something in motion. An uncommitted life doesn't produce anything. Find 1 thing, commit to doing that 1 thing, and keep that promise to yourself. Make a commitment to your life and oneness with God. Challenge your spirit. Don't look to others. Don't be concerned with what others might say about you, because people will talk either way. Invest in you, your goals, your dreams, and your purpose.

It has been proven that the difference between good and great people is that they dedicate 20 minutes each and every day to practicing or doing something towards their goals, dreams, and desires. What have you done today to invest in you?

Take 1 step at a time. But surely, if you stand still, the concerns will not go away. Don't be hard on yourself, everyone gets stuck from time to time. ***Mental shackles are the hardest to break.***

Metanoia awakening is a transformational change in one's life, resulting from repentance and spiritual awareness, prayer, reading God's word, and effort.

When you get sick and tired of being sick and tired, you will begin to take steps to change your current view.

AFFIRMATION:

"I am not stuck. Every day brings new possibilities, and I have the courage to take the next step toward my goals."

PHYSICAL ACTIVITY (GRATITUDE & SELF-LOVE):

Take a 15-minute walk in a place where you feel peaceful. While walking, reflect on one area of your life where you've felt stuck. Imagine that with each step, you are breaking free from what's been holding you back.

MINDFUL EXERCISE:

Write down one small action you can take today to move forward, even if it feels challenging. Commit to doing it, no matter how small it may seem.

BIBLICAL PASSAGE:

"For the Spirit God gave us does not make us timid, but gives us power, love, and self-discipline." — 2 Timothy 1:7

God has equipped you with the strength and courage to push forward. Lean on His power as you take steps toward freedom.

DAY 5

GIVE IN THE MIDST

—⁕—

MORNING CHARGE:

Pay it forward today. Find something you can do, say, or give to show the world a taste of your greatness today.

Reasons and Seasons.

First, you must understand that God's seasons are not the same as our seasons. His thoughts are above our thoughts, so too are His ways above our ways.

Therefore, you don't need to know the whole plan, nor should you, because most of us, if we knew the plan, would get in the way or try to get ahead of God's plan, to force the process.

Trusting God's process is a part of your faith walk in action. Sometimes it's a test, and sometimes it's for training. Usually, it will come in the form of a valley experience, but if you stop to sulk and stew, you will prolong your valley experience. Learn and observe, gain knowledge and wisdom.

Keep pressing toward the mark,

Keep moving towards your goals

Stay prayed up

Stay positive

And most of all, be grateful while going through the process. It is very helpful to attach a positive emotion to your goals. Visualize it, feel it, and see yourself already there. You are being shaped by the Master Potter. Pruned and refined.

Don't focus on the problem while you are in the midst of it.

Instead, find ways:

To serve mankind

Forgive those who have wronged you

To love

To be patient

To just listen

To show kindness

To pray for others …

To give of yourself freely to others even when it seems like you don't have anything to give. The truth is, you do, so give of yourself those things that don't cost money. The act of giving will shift your focus off of the negativity and poor thoughts and onto something positive. The act of giving will also warm your heart, heal you from within, and give you a feeling of peace that you won't understand.

AFFIRMATION:

"Even in difficult times, I have the strength to give, love, and serve others with an open heart."

PHYSICAL ACTIVITY (GIVE KINDNESS):

Spend time doing something kind for someone else today. Whether it's sending an email of appreciation, giving a small gift, or simply offering a listening ear, give with an open heart, a compliment, or a smile.

MINDFUL EXERCISE:

Practice lifting up others and cheering someone else on. It's not about outshining someone because if there was only one shining star in the sky, it would be awfully dark. Reflect on a past difficult time. Journal about how you were able to grow or learn from that experience. This reflection will remind you of your strengths.

BIBLICAL PASSAGE:

> *"Do nothing from selfish ambition or conceit, but in humility count others more significant than yourselves. Let each of you look not only to his own interests, but also to the interests of others"* — Philippians 2:3-4

When you give to others, even when you're going through a tough time, you create space for blessings to flow into your own life.

DAY 6

FINDING THE SILVER LINING

MORNING CHARGE:

If you do nothing, nothing will change.

Don't dwell on the negative or the "why" things are perceived as negative happen to you. Find the "silver lining" and focus on all that is positive in your life instead.

Think about it: negative attracts negative, while positive pulls in positive.

Gratitude is a state of mind and, therefore, a state of being.

Things happen; it's called life. The only way things stop happening is when you are dead. Accept this and move on.

Worrying and dwelling on what has happened does nothing to change what happened. Organize your thoughts and move on.

What is your silver lining? Every situation has a lesson wrapped in it. Every peak and valley has a lesson within it. Every day is an opportunity to learn something new and grow. What is in the picture of your life? At every stage of your life, there should be a picture of what you desire, what you want to accomplish, and a picture of gratitude for where you are and what you have achieved. Have a goal, have a plan, and work on your plan. Picture it. Not everyone can see *your* big picture. Planes fly, but not everyone is a Lear jet; some people are just crop dusters. Your picture is your picture. Some cannot see it, believe in it, or perceive it, and that is ok because it is not their picture; it's yours.

Mental Activity:

Don't tell everyone about your problems. 80% don't care and the other 20 % are just glad it's not their problem. Also, don't share your dream, desire, and purpose with everyone, it's not meant to be understood by all. So, keep it off social media too, until it is fully developed.

Think about this for a moment; Mountains don't rise without an earthquake. But rising tides do lift all ships.

AFFIRMATION:

"I choose to focus on the positive. Every challenge I face holds a lesson that helps me grow."

PHYSICAL ACTIVITY (GRATITUDE & SELF-LOVE):

Stand outside for a few minutes and simply look at the sky. Whether it's sunny or cloudy, take a moment to appreciate the beauty in front of you. This helps cultivate gratitude for what's present, even in life's storms.

MINDFUL EXERCISE:

Write down one positive thing that came from a recent difficulty you faced. It could be a lesson learned, a new perspective, or even the strength you gained. Focus on the silver lining.

BIBLICAL PASSAGE:

> *"And we know that in all things God works for the good of those who love him, who have been called according to his purpose."* — Romans 8:28

God is using everything you go through to shape you for your greater purpose. Trust that even in hardship, good is being worked out in your life.

DAY 7

FEAR OF FAILING

———❦———

MORNING CHARGE:

Get up and try.

We all know the story, but it bears repeating. Grasshoppers are trapped in a glass jar after repeatedly trying to jump out but continuously bumping their head on the lid and falling back into the jar, they will eventually stop jumping. Then one day you take the lid off. The grasshopper can see the sky, but still, for hours, it will not attempt to jump out of the jar for FEAR of failing.

So, know that usually, conditional fear comes from an associated painful situation. God created grasshoppers to hop, so eventually, after looking up at the sky, they will attempt to hop out to freedom.

God did not create you to be fearful, lacking, or lowly. Even if life has dealt you some painful blows, it is in your nature to get up and grab hold of your destiny.

Miracles happen when the unseen becomes the seen. It's when faith is working, and destiny catches up to it in time. It is when that which you dreamed of begins to manifest even better than you could have imagined.

So, leap to your freedom; God created you to have and live in abundance. Look up to the hills from where your help comes from. See God's glory, it's time for you to rise from your fear and pain to freedom.

Keep trying, keep striving. Look up, what do you see? If it is your time to jump. . . then jump.

There is a beautiful world out there waiting for you.

Mental Activity:

What areas of your life do you feel trapped in?

Are you really trapped, or were you trapped but now are not? But you just have not moved.

Fear and Faith cannot reside in your heart at the same time.

Unlock those imaginary boundaries in your mind. *You are created with an unlimited spirit. Challenge yourself. Dare to push yourself to new limits. Usually, what you fear is the worst-case scenario that never even* *happens. How much time have you spent fearing something that never happened? You don't get that time back. So, don't waste any more time wallowing in fear of something that will probably never happen.*

When you open your wings and begin to soar you will begin to see life from a new vantage point. This then will generate new thoughts and ideas and present a new and refreshing view of life.

Rise with gratitude

Rise in stature

Rise in thoughts

Rise in character

Rise in wealth

Rise in the morning full of excitement

Rise on a mission

Rise with a smile!

AFFIRMATION:

"I am not afraid of failure. I see every attempt as a step forward, and I trust God to guide my path."

PHYSICAL ACTIVITY (GRATITUDE & SELF-LOVE):

Go for a 5-minute run or jog. With each step, imagine you're outrunning the fear that has been holding you back. Let the movement symbolize your freedom from fear.

MINDFUL EXERCISE:

Write down an area of your life where fear has kept you from moving forward. Then, take one small step today toward overcoming that fear. This could be as simple as speaking up or trying something new.

BIBLICAL PASSAGE:

> *"Have I not commanded you? Be strong and courageous. Do not be afraid; do not be discouraged, for the Lord your God will be with you wherever you go."* — Joshua 1:9

God is with you, guiding your steps. Fear has no place where faith lives.

DAY 8

SIFTING NOT SHIFTING

MORNING CHARGE:

This comfort zone is not so comfortable... I need to make moves.

Sifting is separating and weeding out impurities through *agitation*. What are mental impurities? Anger, resentment, worry, fear, stress, pressure, procrastination, and anxiety.

When you remove these things from your thoughts, your mind and heart become lighter. Please remember that sometimes the process of getting there is through agitation.

Agitation – friction, going against, rubbing, sifting, shaking up, constant movement back and forth, frustration; patience.

Sifting is the method of removing anger, resentment, pain, troubled thoughts, worry, impurities, doubt, fear, stress, pressure, and feelings of lack. By removing these things, your mind and heart become lighter, but know that the process of getting there is sometimes brought about by agitation; sifting.

Most people's comfort zone is not even comfortable, it may be familiar but not comfortable. It's what you know, not really what you like or approve of, nor is it a state you want to stay in.

Well, then get moving. Do something different to obtain a different outcome. Do more, do less, take a different route, approach it differently, and think about it through a different lens. I used to say I was not a morning person. Then, one day, it hit me that morning comes every day. I made the conscious decision that I will no longer let every morning be an unpleasant experience for me. I chose how I view mornings and what I do in the morning. I added some of my favorite activities. Now, I am a morning, noon, and night person.

AFFIRMATION:

"I release all anger, fear, and resentment. My mind is clear, and my heart is light."

PHYSICAL ACTIVITY (GRATITUDE & SELF-LOVE):

Spend 5 minutes shaking out your body—arms, legs, and shoulders. Let go of any tension or stress you've been holding on to. As you do, imagine releasing all negative energy, making room for positivity.

MINDFUL EXERCISE:

Write down three things that are causing you stress or worry. Next, jot down how you can let go or manage these feelings, even if it means simply trusting that things will get better.

BIBLICAL PASSAGE:

> *"Cast all your anxiety on him because he cares for you."* — 1 Peter 5:7

God is ready to carry your burdens. Let go of your worries and trust in His care.

DAY 9

RIPPLE

MORNING CHARGE:

My choices have consequences.

How fast do you recover?

My epic ripple is not going to let you win. If something or someone disturbs your peace. Be like water when a stone is thrown into it. Let it set off a ripple, but only for a few seconds before your water becomes still again. Surround yourself with positive people. Only let things affect your mood for no more than 3 minutes unless it's something that can affect you for a lifetime.

Come to know your triggers; understand them and why they exist. Evil people will push, press, and hunt for your hot buttons just to get a reaction out of you. If you react for more than 3 minutes, they win. Self-control is the control of oneself and is a great skill to master.

Emotional Intelligence – is the ability to be self-aware and to self-manage your emotions and actions. Ultimately, it is the ability to respond instead of react.

Mental Activity:

Think through it – is it worth it? consider the source, consider their why, and evaluate it in your mind. Then and only then speak, if necessary. If in that moment you feel heated, count to 10 backward. Have a silly song you can sing or play in your head that will move your mood quickly.

Notice your body language. Notice your facial expressions. This takes practice. Celebrate small victories when you exercise control during a situation in which you would not have ordinarily been able to control your words or actions. Consider the importance of the situation and only let it occupy time and space if it is meaningful and impactful to your life, your future, and your livelihood. How you respond matters.

AFFIRMATION:

"I am resilient. When setbacks come, I bounce back stronger and wiser." I respond instead of reacting. I am calm.

PHYSICAL ACTIVITY (GRATITUDE & SELF-LOVE):

Do 10 jumping jacks, each one symbolizing your ability to bounce back from life's challenges. As you jump, repeat the affirmation: "I am resilient. I am calm."

MINDFUL EXERCISE:

Reflect on a recent challenge or disappointment. Write down how you can recover from it and move forward. Focus on the lesson learned rather than the feeling it brought you.

BIBLICAL PASSAGE:

"The righteous may fall seven times, but they rise again" — Proverbs 24:16

No matter how many times you fall, God gives you the strength to rise again. Keep moving forward.

DAY 10
RESILIENCE

‿⟋⟋⟍⟍⟋⟍⟋‿

MORNING CHARGE:

Push yourself in just one area of your life today. Smile while doing it.

Matrix Moves – bob and weave- bounce back but don't let that negative arrow catch you. Don't let negative thoughts creep into your mind, they can sink your ship faster than you think. Talk to yourself, encourage yourself, because sometimes you're all you've got. But guess what, You possess more than enough to lift yourself and your mood.

The mind is designed for survival, while vices are created to alter or numb our consciousness. Vices can take many forms, including alcohol, drugs, sex, noise, intrusive thoughts, isolation, food, social media binging, emotional barriers, video games, or relationships with others. All of these can serve as a means to escape reality.

To avoid relying on external substances or distractions, learn how to self-medicate and regulate your feelings and emotions. Practice sitting alone in a room and find ways to uplift yourself, cheer yourself on, and express gratitude for who you are.

Avoid comparisons, and don't hold yourself to the standards set by others. Value yourself and show yourself respect. Acknowledge your virtues and recognize that you have the right to be happy with who you are. Trust yourself and take charge of your own life. Believe that you are appreciated and complex. Never assume that others are more deserving of happiness than you. Believe in you; dust yourself off. But don't let it stop you from working toward your goals. In my house, a pity party setback can only be 24 hours long. Then you've got to formulate a plan to get back in there and fight, grind, and work on getting past this hurdle. Know that you are stronger and better than this seeming hurdle. They/it cannot stop you!

AFFIRMATION:

"I face challenges with courage and confidence, knowing they make me stronger."

PHYSICAL ACTIVITY (GRATITUDE & SELF-LOVE):

Go outside and take a deep breath of fresh air. Stretch your arms wide, embracing the world around you. As you do, imagine yourself absorbing the strength you need to face today's challenges.

MINDFUL EXERCISE:

Write down one challenge you are currently facing. List three ways you can tackle this challenge with resilience. Focus on what you can control, and trust in the process of growth.

BIBLICAL PASSAGE:

"I can do all things through Christ who strengthens me."
— Philippians 4:13

Remember that with God's strength, you can overcome any obstacle. Lean into that strength today.

DAY 11

THE PRICE OF GREATNESS

—◦⊱❈⊰◦—

MORNING CHARGE:

Be the difference you want to see in others.

Greatness comes at a price, which is rooted in responsibility and integrity. To achieve true greatness, one must embrace the accountability that comes with one's actions and decisions. This journey involves a continuous pursuit of wisdom and understanding, which are essential for navigating life's challenges.

Moreover, cultivating discernment allows us to make thoughtful choices that reflect our values, while good judgment helps us to assess situations effectively. By striving for these qualities, we not only enhance our character but also positively impact those around us. Ultimately, greatness is not just about personal achievement; it is about uplifting others and leading with purpose.

AFFIRMATION:

"I am responsible for my actions and my growth. I seek wisdom, understanding, and integrity in all I do."

PHYSICAL ACTIVITY (GRATITUDE & SELF-LOVE):

Take 5 minutes to do a simple physical task like cleaning or organizing a space in your room. As you do, focus on the satisfaction of responsibility and the clarity it brings.

MINDFUL EXERCISE:

Reflect on a time when you showed great responsibility or integrity. Journal about how it made you feel and how it contributed to your personal growth. Consider what areas of your life need more responsibility and action.

BIBLICAL PASSAGE:

"The integrity of the upright guides them, but the unfaithful are destroyed by their duplicity."
— Proverbs 11:3

True greatness comes from living with integrity and responsibility. Let this guide your actions today.

DAY 12
GRATITUDE AND REFLECTION

———⟨❦⟩———

MORNING CHARGE:

Be patient with yourself because your awesomeness is starting to show.

Gratitude and reflection are powerful tools that can help you see the brighter side of life and grow into the best version of yourself. Gratitude is about appreciating the good things, big or small, in your life, like a kind friend, a sunny day, or even your favorite song. When you take a moment to focus on what you're thankful for, it shifts your perspective, helping you feel happier and less stressed. Reflection, on the other hand, is like hitting the pause button to think about your experiences, choices, and emotions. It allows you to learn from challenges, celebrate victories, and understand yourself better. Together, gratitude and reflection give you the power to turn ordinary moments into something meaningful and help you grow stronger through life's ups and downs.

Imagine starting each day by writing down one thing you're thankful for and ending the day by reflecting on what you learned. These small habits can create a big change. Gratitude keeps you focused on the positive, and reflection helps you learn from everything, both the good and the bad. When things feel tough, reflecting on how you've overcome challenges before can give you the courage to keep going. And when life is good, gratitude reminds you to savor those moments. These practices are not just for now; they're tools you can use for the rest of your life to stay motivated, grounded, and ready to face the future with confidence.

So, create a list of achievements and things you are grateful for, at least 7 things; this can serve as a powerful tool for reflection and personal growth. This exercise helps you acknowledge your progress and appreciate the positives in your life, especially during challenging times.

Revisiting these lists regularly can enhance your emotional well-being and perspective. On tough days, remembering your achievements and the positives in your life can remind you of your journey and growth, fostering a sense of gratitude and spiritual awareness.

AFFIRMATION:

"I am grateful for every experience that has shaped me. I recognize the blessings in my life, both big and small."

PHYSICAL ACTIVITY (GRATITUDE & SELF-LOVE):

Take a short walk and as you do, think of 10 things you are grateful for from the past five years. Focus on how each moment has contributed to your growth.

BIBLICAL PASSAGE:

"Give thanks in all circumstances; for this is God's will for you in Christ Jesus." — 1 Thessalonians 5:18

Gratitude shifts your focus from what you lack to the abundance already present in your life.

DAY 13

EBRACING YOUR UNIQUENESS

MORNING CHARGE:

I am built different and stronger than I thought.

Claim what you desire. Speak it, visualize it, ask God for it, and believe that it will happen.

Ask yourself what is truly important. Why do you want it? Is it a need, a want, or a desire?

Release the imaginary barriers from your mind. If you can dream it, see it, and desire it, then go after it. Dare to push yourself beyond your limits and become unlimited. There is something that you can do better than everyone else. It's your gift from God. Tap into it. Embrace it. Cultivate it. Share your gift with the world. Your style is made up of your life experiences, your choices, your family, your beliefs, and your likes, not social likes.

AFFIRMATION:

"I am proud of who I am. My uniqueness is my strength, and I don't need to change to fit in."

PHYSICAL ACTIVITY (GRATITUDE & SELF-LOVE):

Take a 10-minute walk and focus on how your body moves. Appreciate your individuality, your walk, your pace, and your rhythm. Embrace the fact that you are one of a kind.

MINDFUL EXERCISE:

Write down a situation where you felt pressure to fit in or be like others. Then, write how staying true to yourself is more important. Reflect on the beauty of your uniqueness and how it contributes to the world.

BIBLICAL PASSAGE:

"But you are a chosen people, a royal priesthood, a holy nation, God's special possession, that you may declare the praises

*of him who called you out of darkness into
his wonderful light."* — 1 Peter 2:9

You are unique, chosen by God, and your individuality
is part of His perfect design. Celebrate your uniqueness.

DAY 14

PROTECTION

MORNING CHARGE:

Do not let anyone steal your joy because your joy is valuable, shiny, and looks like gold.

God is in front of you casting a shadow of protection; walk in it. It's called Grace and Mercy. You cannot get over it until you let it go and be honest and let God in. You cannot build a stronger fortress than God. Cast your cares and concerns to Him, and seek God's protection. Write down the things that worry you and throw them away from you. Later, take that paper and rip it into small pieces and throw it away.

AFFIRMATION:

"I walk in God's grace and mercy. I am protected, guided, and loved every step of the way."

PHYSICAL ACTIVITY (GRATITUDE & SELF-LOVE):

Do 10 minutes of stretching or light exercise. As you move, imagine God's grace covering and protecting you, filling you with peace and strength.

MINDFUL EXERCISE:

Reflect on a time when you experienced God's grace in your life. Write about how it felt and how it changed you. If you can, offer grace to someone in your life today by forgiving or being patient.

BIBLICAL PASSAGE:

"Surely goodness and mercy shall follow me all the days of my life, and I will dwell in the house of the Lord forever." — Psalm 23:6

Rest in the knowledge that God's grace and mercy are with you, guiding you and protecting you.

DAY 15
YOUR PAST HAS PASSED

―⸩⸨―

MORNING CHARGE:

How much time have you spent today investing in yourself?

You live in the present. LET GOD RENEW you and give you a totally new mind and heart. But it will require you to trust the process and Him.

Circumstances can make you or break you, they can certainly change you over time, and you wake up one day and say This is not me, why am I acting this way? *Cream doesn't turn your coffee black; it lightens every cup it enters. Just because you are in a dark situation, make up your mind to brighten each situation you face.*

Sometimes missteps happen to guide you in a different direction, away from harm, and create a new avenue to get you to your destiny. Don't fight against the universal plan. Move in flow with your surroundings.

Each day, assess what you have done. How much time have you invested in you, compared to how much time you spend on social media feeds, watching television, and playing video games? At the end of each day, I hope you find that you spent more time investing in yourself than those things that will not move you forward or get you closer to your goals, dreams, and desires. If not, it's time to reassess how and what you spend your time on. Change is something you have to make happen.

AFFIRMATION:

"I release my past and embrace the present. Each day is a fresh opportunity to grow and become who I am meant to be."

PHYSICAL ACTIVITY (GRATITUDE & SELF-LOVE):

Go outside and take deep breaths, focusing on letting go of any burdens from your past. With each exhale, imagine yourself releasing the weight of past mistakes or regrets.

MINDFUL EXERCISE:

Write down something from your past that you've been holding onto. Fold the paper and let it go by tearing it up or burning it safely. This symbolizes releasing the hold the past has on you.

BIBLICAL PASSAGE:

> *"Forget the former things; do not dwell on the past. See, I am doing a new thing!"* — Isaiah 43:18-19

God is constantly working in your life, creating new opportunities. Let go of the past and open your heart to what He has in store for you.

DAY 16
LIKING YOURSELF WITHOUT VALIDATION

❧══❧

MORNING CHARGE:

Tell your inner self. . . you've got this. Swagger is the word for today.

Believe in Yourself. Listen to the quiet whispering voice. . . it's God speaking to you... see with your spiritual eye – you will know because your natural mind cannot understand.

Think about a time when you faced a difficult or negative situation. When someone you look up to speaks negatively about you or to you. When it looked like the odds were stacked against you.

I ask you, who are the people you look up to? Have they ever spoken negatively about you? Who are your Giants?

I think about the story of David and Goliath when David's dad and brother did not believe in him and spoke against him fighting the Philistines.

David knew he had been training for such a battle. He was not afraid because he had to fight Lions and Bears, and God was with him in these battles. David knew God would be with him in this battle, too. You do not have to accept what others say about you as true.

When you are faced with a difficult situation. . .

1. You should **train your mind** to believe what God told you is his plan for you. He put his plan on the inside of you.

2. You should **train your mind** to believe what God told you is his plan for you. He put his plan on the inside of you.

3. Palms 27:1 says
   a. The Lord is my light. . . light (meaning) The lord is your guide in dark places
   b. Whom shall you fear? You don't have to accept those negative words to be true.

4. **Trust God**
   a. You can do all things through Christ. Know your self-worth.

5. **Have Focused Faith** - keep your mind on the positive things God tells you.

6. **Take Courage-** God has prepared you.
   a. At the end of Psalms 27 it says - Remain confident in this YOU will see the Goodness of the Lord. In the land of the living. Even when things look impossible, never let negative thoughts come into your mind.

Think about this. . . ships sink when raging water seeps in. So don't let those raging thoughts seep in.

AFFIRMATION:

"I do not need likes or approval from others to validate my worth. I like who I am just as I am."

PHYSICAL ACTIVITY (GRATITUDE & SELF-LOVE):

Take a break from social media today. Instead of scrolling for validation, spend 10 minutes doing something you love, like drawing, writing, or listening to music. Focus on how it feels to enjoy your own company.

MINDFUL EXERCISE:

Write down three things you like about yourself that have nothing to do with appearance or social approval. Reflect on why these qualities matter more than external validation.

BIBLICAL PASSAGE:

> *"Am I now trying to win the approval of human beings, or of God? Or am I trying to please people? If I were still trying to please people, I would not be a servant of Christ." —* Galatians 1:10

Your value doesn't come from others' opinions but from God. Focus on pleasing Him, not seeking validation from the world.

DAY 17
PRECIOUS TIME

❧～✦～☙

MORNING CHARGE:

What is your Why? Let it motivate you today.

Fear and anxiety are not important enough to use up any more of my thoughts or any more of my time. Not today. Attitude determines your aptitude and altitude. Each one of us is given the same 24 hours. Extraordinary people – find ways to maximize the day. They wake up early and sometimes go to sleep late. So, do not ignore it, avoid it, try to sleep through it; instead, face it head-on, conquer it, and seize the day. And again, the only reason why I was not a morning person before now is because I kept speaking it into my atmosphere. *Now I see beauty in the sunrise just like I do at sunset.* In the world of Six Sigma, there is an exercise where you have to ask yourself "why" seven layers deep. This is where you take the initial why, and go deeper into why that previous why exists. This is not an easy exercise. But sometimes the first few whys are superficial, and it takes those additional deeper whys to uncover the true heart of your why.

MINDFUL EXERCISE:

Seizing the Day

1. **Morning Reflection**: Start your day by setting a clear intention. As soon as you wake up, take five deep breaths and silently affirm:
   - *Today, I choose peace over fear, action over anxiety, and joy over worry.* This affirmation grounds you in the present and helps shift your mindset toward gratitude and purpose.

2. **Gratitude Sunrise**: Spend five minutes observing the morning (even if it's from your window). Focus on the colors, the sounds, and the stillness of the early hours. With each deep breath, name something you're grateful for. This practice helps you see beauty in the morning and reminds you that each day is a gift.

3. **Time Inventory**: At the start of your day, write down one way you can maximize your time. Maybe it's dedicating 30 minutes to a personal goal or choosing to let go of something unproductive. Check in with yourself at the end of the day to reflect on how you spent those precious 24 hours.

BIBLICAL PASSAGE

"She is clothed with strength and dignity; she can laugh at the days to come." — Proverbs 31:25

This verse reminds us to face each day with strength and confidence, free from the grip of fear or anxiety. When you embrace the day with the right mindset, you are better equipped to maximize your time and approach challenges with grace.

DAY 18
REFINEMENT

MORNING CHARGE:

Identify one task you've been procrastinating on and commit to working on it, finishing it today.

There is a verse in Malachi that states, "He will sit as a refiner and purifier of silver."

Puzzled about what this meant a woman went to a Silversmith and asked if she could watch and observe the process of refining silver. The silversmith agreed.

He held a piece of metal over a fire to let it heat up. He explained that when refining silver, you must put it in the middle of the flame where the fire is the hottest to burn away all of the impurities. She thought about the bible verse again, he sat as a refiner like a purifier of silver. She then asked the silversmith, "Is it true that you have to sit there in front of the fire the whole time while the impurities are being removed?" The silversmith replied, yes. He went further to explain that not only must he sit there the whole time, but he must keep his eye on the piece of silver the entire time, while it is in the fire because if the piece is left even a moment too long, the flames could damage it.

The woman remained silent for a while then she asked, how do you know when the piece is fully refined? The silversmith smiled and said, "That's easy, it's when I can see my image in it.

If today, you are feeling the heat of life, just remember that God could be refining you and He is sitting right there with you, holding and watching you, until He can see his image in you.

AFFIRMATION:

"I am more than the number of likes or followers I have. My worth is infinite and unmeasurable."

PHYSICAL ACTIVITY (GRATITUDE & SELF-LOVE):

Go on a 15-minute walk and leave your phone behind. As you walk, think about how much more peaceful life feels without constantly checking for notifications. Appreciate the present moment.

MINDFUL EXERCISE:

At the end of the day, journal about how you felt during your time away from social media.

BIBLICAL PASSAGE:

> *"Do not store up for yourselves treasures on earth, where moths and vermin destroy, and where thieves break in and steal."* —
> Matthew 6:19

DAY 19
BREATHE AND REBOOT

———❦———

MORNING CHARGE:

Love yourself today. . . you deserve it.

Where you spend time focusing is where you will go. Your words and thoughts draw more to you than you know. Sometimes when things don't seem to be working correctly, all you need to do is turn yourself off for a while and then turn yourself back on.

We too must reboot ourselves with rest, relaxation, intimate time with ourselves, pampering oneself, showing self-love, reflection, exercise, quiet time, spend time with nature. Take in slow deep breaths, pray, and meditate, this time allows God to reconnect with your being.

Give yourself a chance to reboot, rebuild, and strengthen your relationship with God.

Give yourself 1 to 2 hours per week, 10 or 15 minutes a day of just pure you time.

Take a long steamy shower. Take a tub bath, with candles. Take a long walk. Love on you each week. Enter into a time of bliss, no worries, no fear, no thoughts, just you and you.

Connect with your inner you, she/he has been waiting to talk to you, so just listen. Be still. Listen to your heartbeat. Breathe out negative thoughts and breathe in positive ones. Breathe out negative habits and breathe in self-love. Breathe out fear and worry and breathe in health and wholeness. Breathe out anger and breathe in self-control and discipline. Breathe out the need to control the outcome and breathe in supernatural outcomes. If your hands are full from holding onto your past, you cannot grasp the future.

AFFIRMATION:

Your brain is your supercomputer, and it runs on the program . . . yourself talk…What you think and what you say can and will affect your day. Speak positive, think positively.

PHYSICAL ACTIVITY (GRATITUDE & SELF-LOVE):

Take 5 minutes to stretch your body. As you stretch, appreciate what your body does for you every day. Thank yourself for showing up, no matter the challenges you've faced.

MINDFUL EXERCISE:

Write a short letter to yourself, expressing love and gratitude for who you are. Focus on your strengths, your journey, and how far you've come. Keep this letter and read it whenever you need a reminder of your worth.

BIBLICAL PASSAGE:

"Love your neighbor as yourself."
— Matthew 22:39

This command reminds us that we must first love ourselves before we can fully love others. Embrace self-love today as a reflection of God's love for you.

DAY 20
BUILDING CONFIDENCE

———⟡———

MORNING CHARGE:

Make today so Epic that yesterday gets jealous!

Confidence is the belief in your abilities, worth, and decisions. It's an inner assurance that, regardless of the challenges you face, you can handle them with courage and determination. Confidence isn't about being perfect or knowing everything; it's about trusting yourself to learn, grow, and adapt.

True confidence comes from self-awareness, understanding your strengths and weaknesses, and embracing both. It's not loud or boastful; instead, it's steady and grounded. Confidence allows you to take risks, step out of your comfort zone, and bounce back from setbacks because you know your value doesn't depend on external validation.

Social media likes and followers are fleeting. Focus on building internal treasures, qualities like kindness, patience, and strength.

AFFIRMATION:

"I trust in my abilities and strengths. I face each day with confidence, knowing I am capable of achieving great things."

PHYSICAL ACTIVITY (GRATITUDE & SELF-LOVE):

Stand tall with your shoulders back and take three deep breaths. As you exhale, visualize releasing any self-doubt. Walk confidently, even if it's just across the room, with the mindset that you are unstoppable.

MINDFUL EXERCISE:

List one or two goals you want to achieve. Then, write down three reasons why you believe you can reach these goals. Focus on your strengths and capabilities. Reflect on past successes that prove you are capable.

BIBLICAL PASSAGE:

"For the Spirit God gave us does not make us

timid, but gives us power, love and self-discipline." — 2 Timothy 1:7

God has equipped you with strength and confidence. Walk boldly in the power He has given you. Tell your problems just how big your God is.

DAY 21
BEWARE OF THE ENERGY TRANSFER

———⟡———

MORNING CHARGE:

I have an INDOMITABLE spirit!

"Be very careful, this one is sneaky".

This can come in the form of subtle or direct and can even happen from superficial contact or interaction. When someone is in a negative state of mind, sometimes they look for another individual to dump that negative energy onto. You know the adage misery loves company, well this is more like, I am upset so I want you to be upset too. I hurt so I want you to hurt too. Someone pissed me off, so here you go – I am looking for a pity party, an amen corner, so to speak. We all know a negative person, just being around them too long, or in dialogue with them for too long seems to bring you down. For this reason, be careful who you invite into your home.

In this situation, you must be strong and conscious of what is happening because it usually will catch you off guard. So immediately after it happens, assess how you feel, and how you felt before the interaction, and work to get back to your peace – **without** transferring that negative energy to someone else!

Immediately once you identify and recognize what has happened, release it back into the atmosphere. Acknowledge that it has happened. Speak to it, tell it, that it cannot stay because there is no room for it in your life. Yes – personification works well in this instance. Sometimes you may need to physically open a door or window, in the act of letting it out. Take a bath, wash it off. Pray it leaves you and shift your focus on something you are grateful for, a gratitude list, and review your goals. Purge it.

In the future, assess yourself before engaging with these types of people. Do you have your shield ready or are you a bit vulnerable and need to avoid them right now? Toxic people and toxic environments are just that toxic. Sometimes they cannot be avoided, so create daily flushes, and shields to remove and prevent toxicity.

AFFIRMATION:

"I am open to new possibilities and choose to see challenges as opportunities to grow. I embrace change and adapt with ease."

PHYSICAL ACTIVITY (GRATITUDE & SELF-LOVE):

Go for a short walk outside. As you walk, reflect on three things in your life that you are thankful for today. Feel gratitude with each step you take.

MINDFUL EXERCISE:

Spend 2-3 minutes standing in front of a mirror. Look yourself in the eyes, and as you do, compliment yourself on something deeper than your appearance. Tell yourself, "I see your strength," or "I value your perseverance."

BIBLICAL PASSAGE:

> *"Do not conform to the pattern of this world but be transformed by the renewing of your mind."* — Romans 12:2

Reflect on how you can change your mindset to overcome today's obstacles.

DAY 22
YOU ARE ENOUGH

—◦◦◦◦◦—

MORNING CHARGE:

Shoulders back, head up, walk with confidence, confident in you, you are (in Yoda's voice)

Know your worth. You are not defined by others. You were created for a great purpose.

You are defined by God, in time even before you were born. Think about that. Your destiny was predestined. Your actions can delay it or detain it, but not even you can stop it.

You are not defined by your mother or your father, not by your former or current address, and not by your income, or the number of likes you receive on social media.

So, stop associating your worth with unworthy things. You are also not defined by your boyfriend or girlfriend, or the lack thereof.

Your worth is defined by God, and it is beautiful just as it is. Strive to show the world how amazing you can be. Focus on becoming the best version of yourself. Love yourself right where you are now and commit to working on yourself every day; mentally, physically, and spiritually. Don't chase perfection as others define it; instead, aim to be the best version of yourself today.

No one else can define you unless you let them.

Don't sell yourself short, for a kind word or money, dinner, or a compliment. Just because you have not been told you are beautiful in a long time doesn't mean that the first person who says it deserves your body in exchange. Don't long for love and attention so badly that you give up something sacred, your body to it. Know your worth.

You are more than just your flesh; your spirit and soul reside in you too. If you are willing to believe it, the Holy Spirit dwells within you too. These three will exist in harmony or be in constant struggle, depending on how you treat you.

Whenever there is discomfort in your body one or more of them are at odds or against some action you are taking/ some decision you are making, or some thought you are having, and it's God's way of warning you that you are about to lower your self-worth.

Listen to your mind, gut, and heart, they are there to help you through your life choices.

Outside influences are just that, outside, you can choose what you let in.

AFFIRMATION:

"I am enough, just as I am. I don't need to prove my worth to anyone."

PHYSICAL ACTIVITY (GRATITUDE & SELF-LOVE):

Do 5 minutes of deep breathing. With each inhale, remind yourself, "I am enough." With each exhale, release any doubts or insecurities about needing external approval.

MINDFUL EXERCISE:

Write a list of accomplishments or moments in your life that made you proud, regardless of whether others noticed or validated them. Focus on what these achievements mean to you, not to others.

BIBLICAL PASSAGE:

> *"For we are God's handiwork, created in Christ*
> *Jesus to do good works, which God prepared*
> *in advance for us to do."* — Ephesians 2:10

God created you with purpose. You are enough, and your value is beyond any external measure.

DAY 23

DISCONNECT TO RECONNECT

—❦—

MORNING CHARGE:

You are awesome, and you piss greatness.

The concept of recharging oneself is vital for personal well-being and emotional health. Just as electronic devices require power to function optimally, humans need to replenish their energy and mental resources to thrive. In our fast-paced, often overwhelming lives, we can become drained by constant demands and stress. It's important to recognize the signs of fatigue and prioritize self-care to restore our physical and mental balance.

Here are some ways to achieve this:

Rest and Sleep. Quality sleep helps to improve cognitive function, emotional well-being, and overall health.

Establishing a nighttime routine, creating a comfortable sleep environment, and ensuring you get enough restful sleep can significantly enhance your energy levels.

Meditation and Mindfulness: Engaging in meditation or mindfulness practices allows you to slow down and focus your thoughts. These practices can reduce stress, improve concentration, and promote a sense of calm.

Connection with Nature: Nature has a remarkable ability to rejuvenate the spirit. The sights, sounds, and smells of nature have a grounding effect, reminding us of the beauty in the world around us.

Physical Activity: Engaging in physical activities like dancing, and hiking not only benefits your physical health but also releases endorphins, the body's natural mood lifters.

Mindful Observation: Taking the time to observe small moments—like watching a leaf fall or catching a snowflake—can foster a deeper appreciation for life's beauty. This practice encourages mindfulness, allowing you to be present and to experience life more fully.

Play and Laughter: Laughter has a unique way of lifting our spirits. It's important to find time for playful moments, whether it's a spontaneous dance in the living room or sharing jokes with friends.

Incorporating these practices into your routine can significantly enhance your overall well-being.

Remember that taking time for yourself is not selfish; it's necessary for maintaining a balanced life. By prioritizing moments of rest, connection, and creativity, you empower yourself to face daily challenges with renewed energy and a positive outlook.

AFFIRMATION:

"By disconnecting from social media, I reconnect with myself. I am whole and complete without external approval."

PHYSICAL ACTIVITY (GRATITUDE & SELF-LOVE):

Turn off your phone for an hour today and spend that time doing something that fills you with joy—whether it's reading, cooking, or exercising. Focus on how it feels to be free from distractions.

MINDFUL EXERCISE:

Reflect on how social media impacts your thoughts about yourself. Journal about how you can create a healthier relationship with it, ensuring that it doesn't define your self-worth.

BIBLICAL PASSAGE:

> *"Set your minds on things above, not on earthly things."* — Colossians 3:2

Keep your focus on what truly matters—your inner growth, values, and the purpose God has given you.

DAY 24

SELF-LOVE OVER SOCIAL MEDIA LOVE

MORNING CHARGE:

I am beginning to see the change in myself, and I like it.

In a world where social media is constantly buzzing, it's easy to feel like your worth depends on the likes, shares, and comments you receive. But here's the truth: real love, the kind that truly fills you up, can't be measured by a notification. Self-love is about seeing your value, not through a filter or someone else's approval, but through the way you treat yourself every day. It's about choosing your happiness over the pressure to look perfect online. Social media love is fleeting, but self-love is a lifelong connection you build with yourself.

You are more than the moments you share online. You are your laughter, your dreams, your struggles, and your victories; all of these are part of who you've become. When you start showing yourself the kindness, care, and understanding you deserve, you'll realize that no amount of likes can ever compare to the love you already carry inside.

Actionable Tips for Prioritizing Self-Love

1. **Follow with Intention**: Curate your feed so it inspires you—unfollow accounts that make you feel like you're not enough.

2. **Turn Criticism into Compassion**: When you feel tempted to compare yourself to someone online, remind yourself that everyone has struggles you can't see. Celebrate your path instead.

3. **Post with Purpose**: If you share online, let it be from a place of joy and authenticity, not because you're seeking validation.

4. **Celebrate Private Wins**: Do things that make you proud but don't feel the need to share them. Your accomplishments are just as valuable without an audience.

Mental Exercise: Social Media Detox Journal

- **Step 1**: Take a break from social media for 24 hours.

- **Step 2**: During the detox, keep a journal and reflect on questions like:
  - How do I feel without the urge to check my phone?
  - What am I noticing about myself or my surroundings?
  - What do I usually turn to social media for, and how can I give that to myself in a healthier way?

- **Step 3**: At the end of the detox, write down one thing you learned about self-love during your break from social media.

Affirmations to Replace Social Media Validation

- *I don't need likes to like myself.*
- *I am proud of who I am, whether anyone sees it or not.*
- *I am valuable because of what's in my heart, not what's on my feed.*
- *I choose to nurture my inner world more than my online presence.*

AFFIRMATION:

"My self-love is stronger than the need for social media approval. I love who I am without needing likes."

PHYSICAL ACTIVITY (GRATITUDE & SELF-LOVE):

Stand in front of a mirror and say, "I love myself" three times. Say it confidently and notice how it feels to affirm yourself without needing anyone else's approval.

MINDFUL EXERCISE:

Think of a time when you felt good about yourself without posting it on social media. Write about that moment and reflect on how it felt to keep that happiness for yourself.

BIBLICAL PASSAGE:

> *"The Lord does not look at the things people look at. People look at the outward appearance, but the Lord looks at the heart."*
> — 1 Samuel 16:7

God values your heart and soul, not the image you portray to the world. Focus on nurturing your inner self.

DAY 25
DISCIPLINE OVER DISTRACTIONS

MORNING CHARGE:

Today is no distraction day. . . focus, I said focus.

The new terms everyone's using are "going down the rabbit hole" and "swipe coma". On average, people spend over three hours each day watching reels, scrolling through threads, chatting, or creating content. Three hours or more! Imagine what you could achieve with that time if you dedicated it to developing your mind, body, and spirit. You could learn a new skill, develop a trade, start a side hustle, drive for Uber, or hit the gym with just one of those three hours.

It's so easy to get lost in time, and you look up and hours have gone by. Someone sends you a funny or relatable thread, or link to a story, and then, two hours later… You gotta set boundaries, alarms, and something to help you regain control of your time. The algorithm knows what you like and will keep sending you things based on what you like and love. If you ever find that you are getting weird junk (I'll let you define what "junk" is for you) observe what you are liking, loving and watching. 6G can read your thoughts and listen in on your conversations, so know that you must mind your words and thoughts too. Yes, frequencies, can pick up on your words and thoughts. I know you have experienced it with ads on your mobile devices.

As a starting point, this week, discipline yourself by limiting your screen time to just 1.5 hours for personal growth. Choose one of your goals, or desires, or just focus on yourself. Alternatively, spend those 90 minutes pursuing, developing, training, working, meditating, or reading something that will make you stronger, better, wealthier, healthier, and wiser.

AFFIRMATION:

"My value is immeasurable. It is not determined by social media likes or others' opinions."

PHYSICAL ACTIVITY (GRATITUDE & SELF-LOVE):

Take a short break from social media today. Instead, spend time journaling or reflecting on what gives your life meaning. Focus on what makes you valuable beyond any digital interaction. If you must - set a social media timer, today I will only spend one hour scrolling, when the timer/ alarm goes off, STOP. Dedicate time to one of your goals.

MINDFUL EXERCISE:

Write down three things that make you valuable, not based on anyone else's approval but on who you are at your core. These might be qualities like kindness, generosity, or creativity.

BIBLICAL PASSAGE:

> "So do not fear, for I am with you; do not be
> dismayed, for I am your God. I will
> strengthen you and help you; I will uphold
> you with my righteous right hand." — Isaiah
> 41:10

Your strength and worth come from God. You don't need others to tell you that you're valuable—you already are.

DAY 26

APPROVAL FROM WITHIN

—⁂—

MORNING CHARGE:

I am, and I feel unshakeable.

The idea of breaking free from external validation. Explore building self-trust, celebrating personal achievements, and cultivating a sense of inner peace by honoring one's true self. Approval from within begins when you stop seeking permission to be yourself and start embracing the person you already are. It's about knowing that your worth isn't tied to anyone else's opinions, but to the quiet confidence that comes from being true to yourself. Imagine the freedom of no longer needing to prove anything to anyone—of standing tall in your uniqueness, flaws, and all. Instead of asking, *What will they think of me?* start asking, *What do I think of myself?* That shift is where real self-esteem begins to grow.

Building inner approval takes time, celebrate your small wins, speak kindly to yourself, and honor the qualities that make you, *you.* Whenever self-doubt creeps in, remind yourself: *I am my own cheerleader.* Spiritual practices like mindfulness, journaling, or meditation can help you reconnect with your inner voice and tune out the noise of the world. When you nurture your own approval, you'll discover a truth that will carry you through any challenge: the only person who truly needs to believe in you, is *you.*

AFFIRMATION:

"I approve of myself. I don't need external validation because I know who I am."

PHYSICAL ACTIVITY (SELF-LOVE):

Mindfulness – select three goals/desires. Every time a negative thought creeps into your mind; laugh at it. Then, replace the thought with an affirmation that will get you closer to that goal or desire. "That's another A grade", "that's another five pounds lost", "that's another outstanding performance at _____". Ground yourself in the understanding that your worth is inherent. You will be surprised at how often negative thoughts try to hijack your self-esteem.

MINDFUL EXERCISE:

Reflect on a time when you sought approval from others. Now, write down how you can give yourself that approval. Affirm your decisions, actions, and path in life.

BIBLICAL PASSAGE:

> *"Fear of man will prove to be a snare, but whoever trusts in the Lord is kept safe."* — Proverbs 29:25

Trust in yourself and in God's plan for you. Seeking approval from others can lead to insecurity, but trusting in God's approval brings peace.

DAY 27

LETTING GO OF COMPARISONS

~~~◦✦◦~~~

MORNING CHARGE:

I release the need to compare myself to others.

The need for likes on social media often stems from a deeper desire to feel seen, valued, and accepted. But true worth doesn't come from numbers on a screen; it comes from knowing who you are and recognizing that you are already enough. Instead of seeking validation from others, focus on the infinite value you hold simply by being you. Social media only shows a highlight reel of people's lives, it's not the full picture. Remember, your journey is yours alone, beautifully unique and incomparable to anyone else's.

A powerful way to let go of the need for likes is to shift your focus inward. Ask yourself: *Am I posting to share joy, creativity, or connection, or is it just to seek approval?* When you create for yourself and not for others, your self-esteem becomes grounded in your authentic self, not in external applause. Try this mantra: *I am worthy as I am, beyond likes, followers, or filters.* Let it remind you that your value can't be measured in hearts or comments because it comes from something much deeper: your spirit, your kindness, and the light only you can bring to the world.

AFFIRMATION:

" My journey is unique, and I trust where I am headed."

PHYSICAL ACTIVITY (GRATITUDE & SELF-LOVE):

Stretch for 5 minutes, and as you do, imagine releasing all comparisons to others. Let go of the tension and pressure to keep up with anyone but yourself.

MINDFUL EXERCISE:

Write down three things that make your life special and unique, apart from anyone else. Focus on your personal journey and remind yourself that no two paths are the same.

BIBLICAL PASSAGE:

> *"Each one should test their own actions. Then*
> *they can take pride in themselves alone,*
> *without comparing themselves to someone*
> *else."* — Galatians 6:4

God has a unique path for you. Embrace your individuality without comparing your journey to others.

DAY 28
I 'LIKE" ME

───※───

MORNING CHARGE: I LIKE ME, IN FACT; I LOVE ME!

Imagine if every day you woke up and hit the "like" button on yourself, not because of how you look or what you've accomplished, but just because you're *you*. That's the kind of like that truly matters: the one that comes from within. Sure, it's nice to get likes online, but what if you started living for the moments that make *you* smile? The times you laugh so hard your stomach hurts, the way you show up for your friends or the quiet pride you feel when you try something new. These are the moments worth "liking" about yourself.

Liking yourself doesn't mean you're perfect, it means you're human. It's about learning to appreciate your quirks, embracing your flaws, and celebrating the person you're becoming. So, as you close this book, remember you don't need anyone else to validate you. You've got the power to "like" yourself every single day. **Say it out loud:** *I like me. I like my heart, my mind, and all the things that make me, me.* When you start liking yourself from the inside out, you'll realize that the world's likes are just a bonus because you've already hit the most important "like" of all.

Let's take it a step further,

Imagine waking up every day and hitting not just the "like" button on yourself, but the "love" button. The kind of love that says, *I'm proud of who I am, no matter what today brings.* Loving yourself is a bold step, bigger than likes or comments because it's about embracing all of you: the strengths, the struggles, and everything in between. It's saying, *I don't just like me; I love me,* and that kind of love radiates far beyond any post or profile.

Once you've fallen in love with yourself, you'll realize something magical: you don't have to seek followers, because *you* are your own best follower. You trust yourself, you walk your own path, and you cheer yourself on. And when it comes to sharing your light with the world, you do it because *you want to,* not because you need approval. You have the power to choose when and how you share yourself, whether it's with a close friend, a project you're passionate about, or an exciting post. It's your decision because your worth is not defined by anyone else's attention. Here is a challenge: every morning, before you check your notifications, take a moment to check in with *you*. Ask yourself, *What do I love about me today?* Follow your dreams before following anyone else, and share your energy when it feels right, knowing you are already whole. The world doesn't need the "filtered" you, we need the real you, the one who knows their value comes from within.

And when you step into that power, when you love, follow, and share yourself authentically, you'll see that you're not just living for the likes. You're living for *you!*

AFFIRMATION:

"I am authentic and true to myself. I don't need to present a version of myself to please others."

PHYSICAL ACTIVITY (GRATITUDE & SELF-LOVE):

Spend 5 minutes dancing or moving to your favorite music. Dance freely, without worrying about how it looks or what anyone else thinks. Embrace the joy of being authentically you.

MINDFUL EXERCISE:

Journal about a time when you felt the pressure to present a certain image online. Reflect on how you can live more authentically, both online and in real life, without feeling the need to filter who you are.

BIBLICAL PASSAGE:

"For you created my inmost being you knitted me together in my mother's womb." — Psalm 139:13

God created you authentically and beautifully. You don't need to change who you are to fit anyone else's expectations.

Now try writing your thoughts for the next 3 days.

BONUS DAY 1

FINDING PEACE IN SOLITUDE

———— ⚜ ————

AFFIRMATION:

"I find peace in my own company. I am whole, even when I am alone."

PHYSICAL ACTIVITY (GRATITUDE & SELF-LOVE):

Spend 15 minutes alone in a peaceful environment, without distractions. Whether it's sitting in a quiet room, by a window, or in nature, focus on your breath and how it feels to simply be present with yourself.

MINDFUL EXERCISE:

Write about how being alone makes you feel. If it feels uncomfortable, reflect on why. Consider how solitude can help you grow and connect more deeply with yourself. Find one positive thing about being alone that you can embrace.

BIBLICAL PASSAGE:

"Be still, and know that I am God." — Psalm 46:10

Solitude offers a space to connect with God and yourself. In moments of stillness, you find peace, strength, and clarity.

WRITING EXERCISE

MY THOUGHTS FOR TODAY

BONUS DAY 2

FINDING PEACE IN SOLITUDE

———◦◦———

AFFIRMATION:

"I enjoy my own company. I am comfortable with who I am and cherish moments of solitude."

PHYSICAL ACTIVITY (GRATITUDE & SELF-LOVE):

Take yourself on a solo date—go for a walk, grab a coffee, or do something you enjoy, just for you. Focus on how it feels to spend quality time with yourself, appreciating your own company.

MINDFUL EXERCISE:

Reflect on a time when you felt lonely and how that moment shaped your relationship with yourself. Now, write about how you can reframe loneliness into an opportunity to grow and connect with your thoughts, dreams, and goals.

BIBLICAL PASSAGE:

> *"The Lord your God is with you, the Mighty Warrior who saves. He will take great delight in you; in his love, he will no longer rebuke you, but will rejoice over you with singing."* — Zephaniah 3:17

You are never truly alone. God rejoices over you, and His presence is always with you, offering comfort and strength in times of solitude.

WRITING EXERCISE
MY THOUGHTS FOR TODAY

BONUS DAY 3

FINDING PEACE IN SOLITUDE

AFFIRMATION:

"I am strong and complete in myself. I do not need others to define my happiness or worth."

PHYSICAL ACTIVITY (GRATITUDE & SELF-LOVE):

Spend 10 minutes meditating or sitting quietly. During this time, affirm that you are enough, just as you are. Imagine yourself as a tree, grounded and unshaken, thriving in solitude. Feel the strength that comes from within.

MINDFUL EXERCISE:

Journal about what it means to be alone but not lonely. Reflect on how solitude can help you hear your inner voice and strengthen your sense of self. Write down one lesson you've learned about yourself during your time alone.

BIBLICAL PASSAGE:

>*"The Lord will fight for you; you need only to be still."* — Exodus 14:14

In solitude, God fights your battles. There is strength in stillness, and you can trust that God is with you, even in your quietest moments.

>*Every day is an opportunity for wonder, and I'm all in for the adventure! I'm prepared to embrace each moment and show up for myself fully!*

WRITING EXERCISE
MY THOUGHTS FOR TODAY

ABOUT INGRID JAMES

With over 23 years of expertise in Operational Excellence and eight years in Supply Chain Management, Ingrid James has built a distinguished career leading large-scale project and implementation initiatives. Her ability to drive complex projects from concept to execution has made her a trusted leader across multiple sectors. Ingrid is currently serving as the Director and Solutions Architect for a SaaS Vendor Management Solution. She pioneers innovative solutions in procurement and supply chain management, providing consultative services and visibility for small businesses across the United States.

A graduate of Florida State University, Ingrid holds a degree in Business Finance with a minor in Accounting. She is Project Management Certified and Six Sigma Yellow Belt Certified, with extensive experience managing nearshore and offshore BPO operations. Her global leadership has taken her to Toronto and St. Catharine, Canada, and Mumbai, India, overseeing large-scale implementations.

Beyond her corporate achievements, Ingrid has a deep-rooted passion for mentorship and community service. She served for eight years in the Gwinnett Football League, including two years as Vice President of the board, and coached as a Defensive Coordinator for three years. Her dedication to personal excellence extended into the fitness world, where she excelled as a professional bodybuilder and personal trainer, winning 1st place in the Atlanta Championship (1999), 1st place in the Georgia Championship (2000), and 2nd place in the Southeast Regionals (2001).

Ingrid's natural exhorter skills led her to become a prominent public speaker, mentoring students at Norcross High School, guiding women through the Gwinnett Department of Children and Family Services, and empowering survivors of human trafficking by teaching essential life skills in resume writing, interviewing, and personal & professional development.

Ordained as a Minister in 2011 through the New Zion Christian Church, where she has been an active serving member since 2001. Ingrid continues to uplift and transform lives through faith, mentorship, health and fitness coaching, and leadership. In recognition of her contributions, she was inducted into the prestigious Marquis Who's Who in America in 2025.

With a lifelong commitment to empowerment, resilience, and transformation, Ingrid now shares her wisdom and experiences through this book, offering a 28-day journey to self-love, confidence, and renewal.

www.ingramcontent.com/pod-product-compliance
Lightning Source LLC
Chambersburg PA
CBHW021335090426
42742CB00008B/613